ANI AFSHAR

BEADED FANTASIES
Ribbon Jewelry

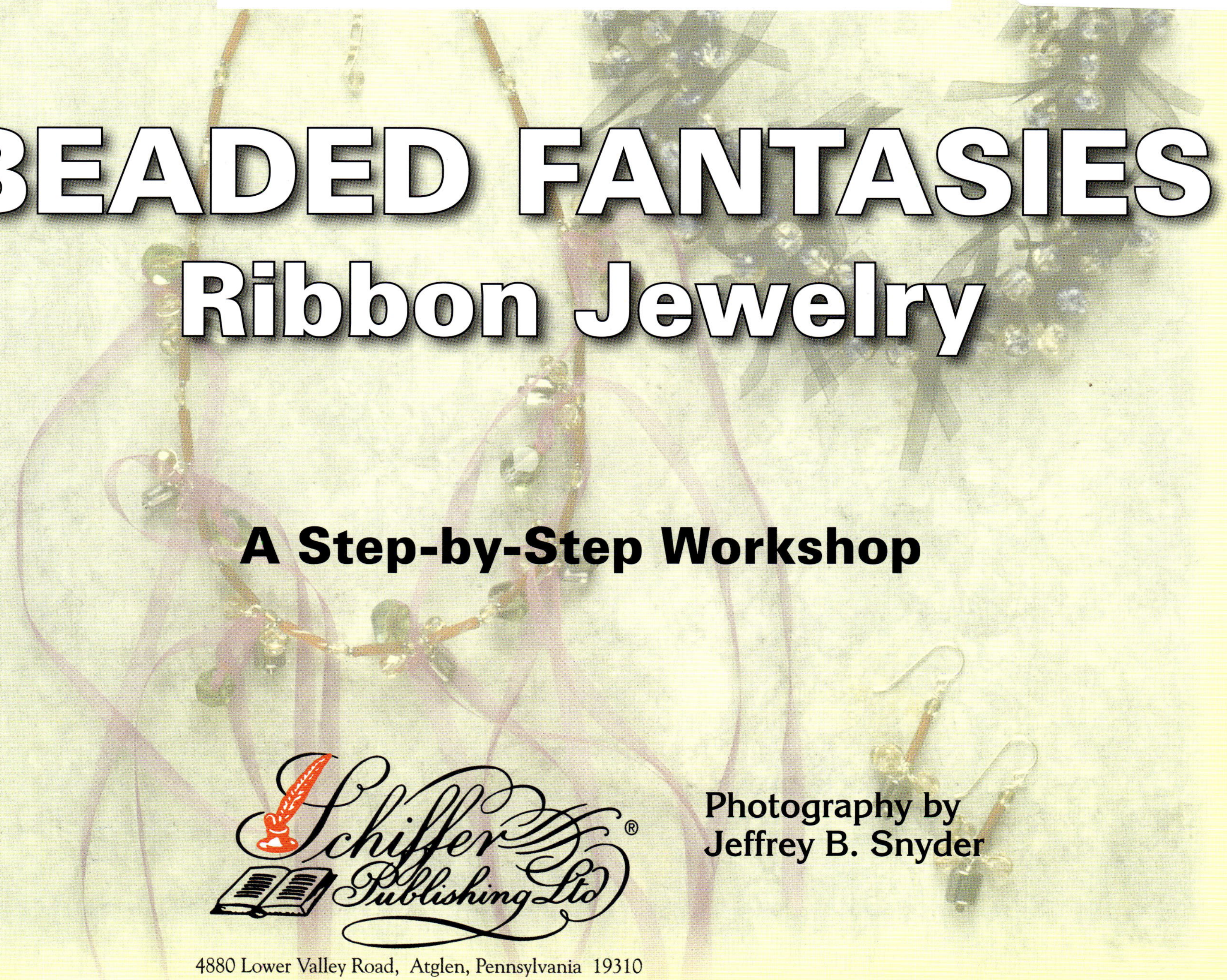

A Step-by-Step Workshop

Photography by
Jeffrey B. Snyder

Schiffer Publishing Ltd®
4880 Lower Valley Road, Atglen, Pennsylvania 19310

Foreword

Integrity is the word that comes to mind when I think of the work of ANI AFSHAR. I've met and worked with many, many artists, and designers over the years – rarely have I come across someone with such clear and focused design intention.

Using bead, wire, fiber, and ribbon, Ani creates a very special vocabulary of texture and volume. The reductive silhouettes that she creates often belie the intricate and precise nature of her technique. As a designer myself, I am in awe of the hand agility required in this medium. Ani is the master.

The craft of weaving and bead manipulation is an ancient one. Ani employs this sense of history and, at the same time, succeeds in creating a very contemporary sensibility. Make no mistake - Ani Afshar is a modernist.

I feel honored to have ANI AFSHAR'S work as part of the selection at my business.

—Gregory Reeves

In May of 2006, Gregory Reeves opened a retail boutique in the heart of the Greenwich Village neighborhood of New York City – ***christopher19design collective***.

Other Schiffer Books by Ani Afshar:
Beading Necklaces with Ani Afshar
Beads & Wires Jewelry
Beads & Strings Jewelry
Beaded Flowers Jewelry

Library of Congress Control Number: 2007943571

Designed by Mark David Bowyer
Type set in Zurich Blk BT / Korinna BT

ISBN: 978-0-7643-2856-5
Printed in China

Schiffer Books are available at special discounts for bulk purchases for sales promotions or premiums. Special editions, including personalized covers, corporate imprints, and excerpts can be created in large quantities for special needs. For more information contact the publisher:

Published by Schiffer Publishing Ltd.
4880 Lower Valley Road
Atglen, PA 19310
Phone: (610) 593-1777; Fax: (610) 593-2002
E-mail: Info@schifferbooks.com

For the largest selection of fine reference books on this and related subjects, please visit our web site at **www.schifferbooks.com**
We are always looking for people to write books on new and related subjects. If you have an idea for a book please contact us at the above address.

This book may be purchased from the publisher.
Include $3.95 for shipping.
Please try your bookstore first.
You may write for a free catalog.

In Europe, Schiffer books are distributed by
Bushwood Books
6 Marksbury Ave.
Kew Gardens
Surrey TW9 4JF England
Phone: 44 (0) 20 8392-8585; Fax: 44 (0) 20 8392-9876
E-mail: info@bushwoodbooks.co.uk
Website: www.bushwoodbooks.co.uk
Free postage in the U.K., Europe; air mail at cost.

Contents

Long Ribbons Necklace

We are making a beaded choker with narrow organza ribbons cascading like feathers.

Here is the bead color palette and the ribbon you will need to complete the first project.

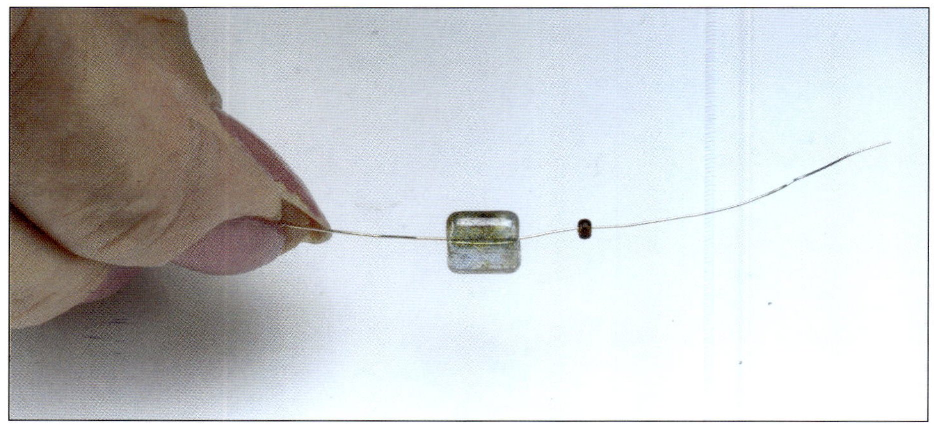

To begin, we're going to make some bead drops to use in the necklace. Place these two beads on 26-gauge wire.

Fold the wire back around the small bead ...

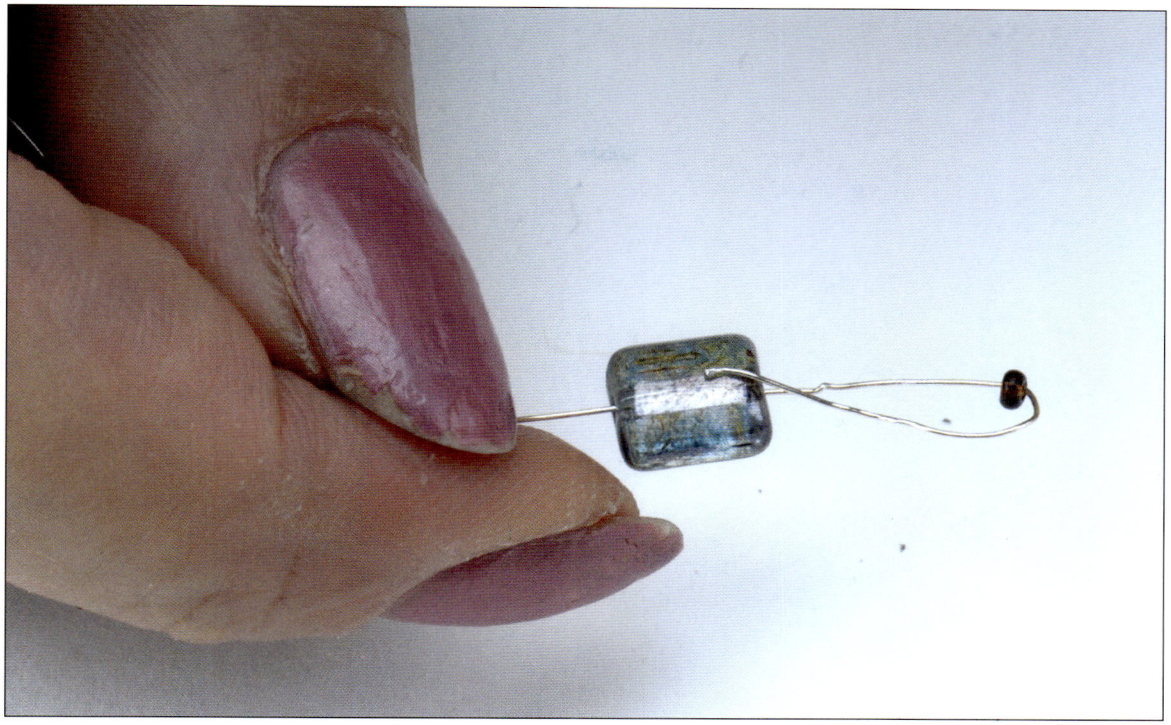

Thread both ends of the folded wire back through the large bead and pull tight. The small bead will secure the wire in place against the larger bead. Use round nosed pliers to create a loop with the wire at the opposite end of the large bead. Twist the wire around the base of the loop to secure it in place.

Use cutters to snip away the excess wire and your first bead drop is complete.

Here are eight identical bead drops for the necklace.

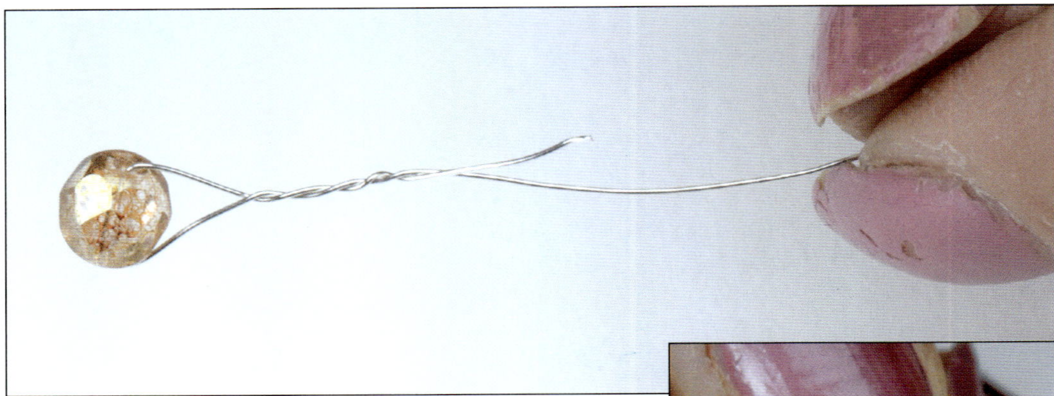

Fold wire around the round pink bead and twist the wire together to secure the bead.

Use your round nosed pliers to create a loop, wrapping the wire around the base of the loop to secure it in place.

Snip loose the excess wire. Here are several of the pink bead drops.

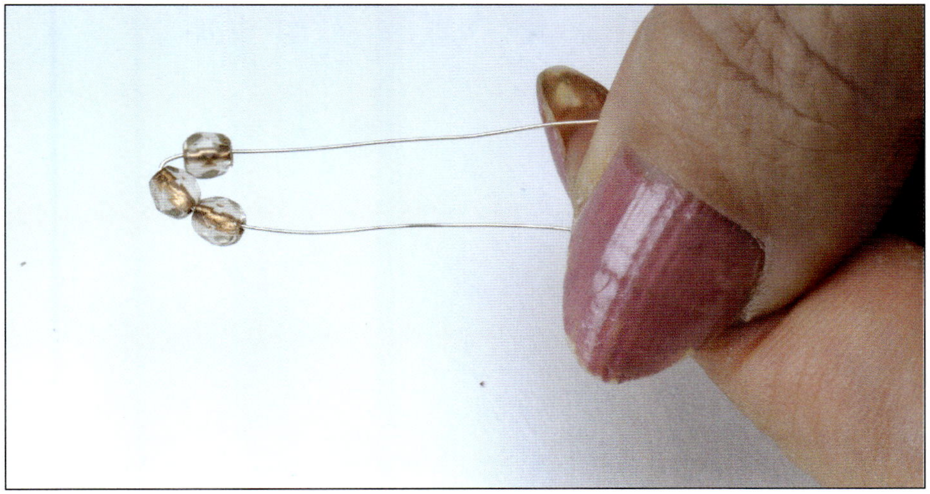

To create a three bead drop, start by stringing 3 beads and folding the wire.

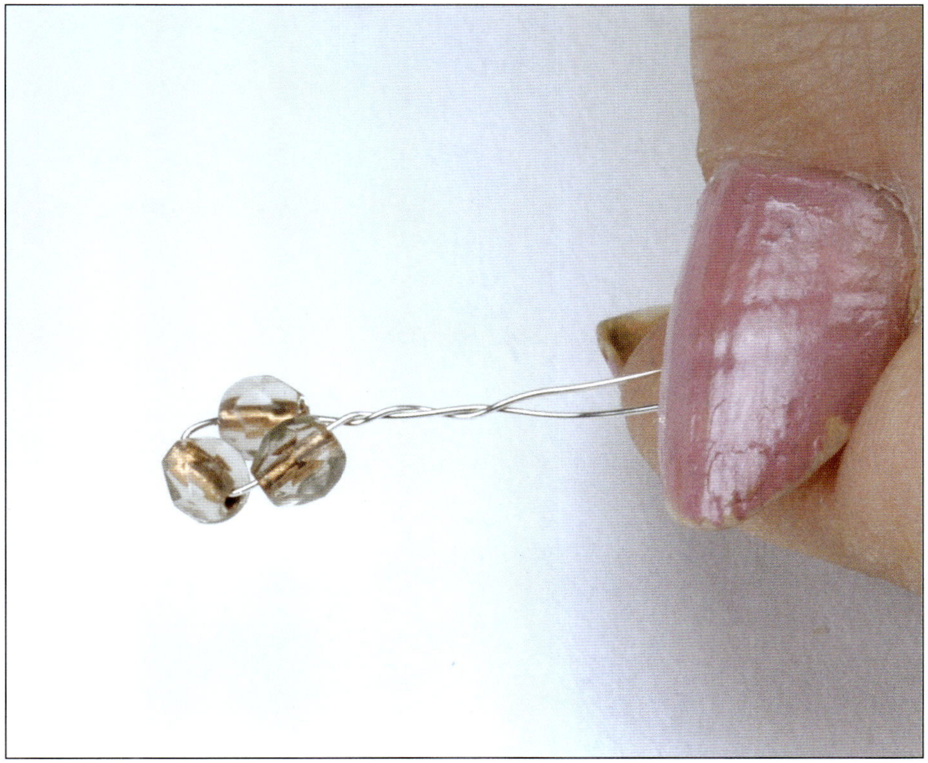

Twist the two wire ends to secure the beads.

Create the loop as before.

Seven finished three bead drops.

Thread the ribbon through your needle.

Thread seven beads with the needle onto the ribbon. Don't cut the ribbon from the spool at this time.

Double knot the bead to the ribbon.

Like so.

Now, tightly double knot the beaded ribbon to a round object like this thick pen shaft. It is important that these are nice, tight knots.

Once the bead is knotted to the shaft, extend a trail of ribbon and cut it loose.

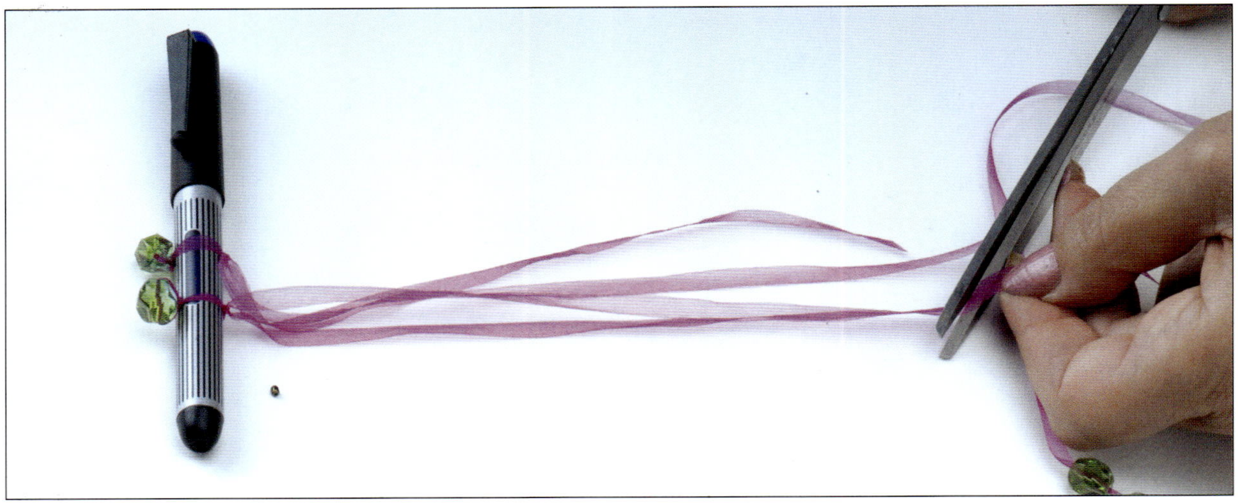

All seven ribboned beads are now on the shaft.

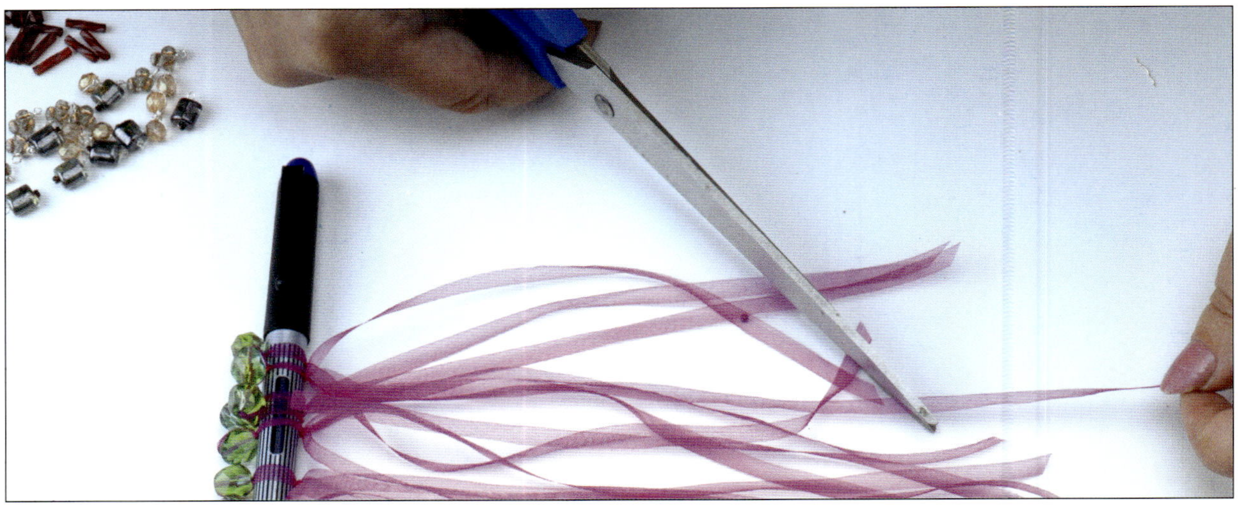

Cut the ribbons to the same length, cutting diagonally across each ribbon so it will not fray.

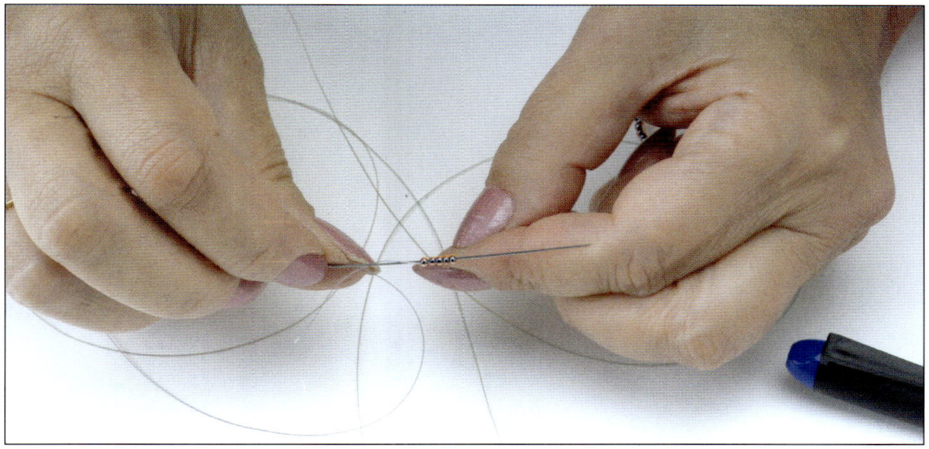

Thread five seed beads onto your needle and monofilament line, making sure to leave about 5" extra monofilament to use to attach the clasps.

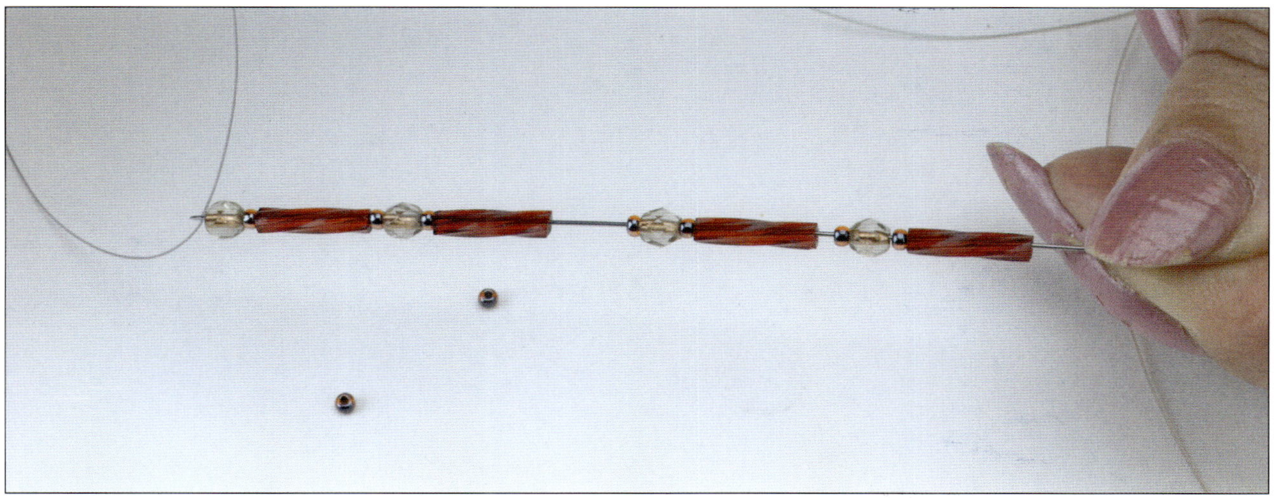

Once the five seed beads are in place, start threading beads in this pattern.

Remove the ribbon beads from the shaft.

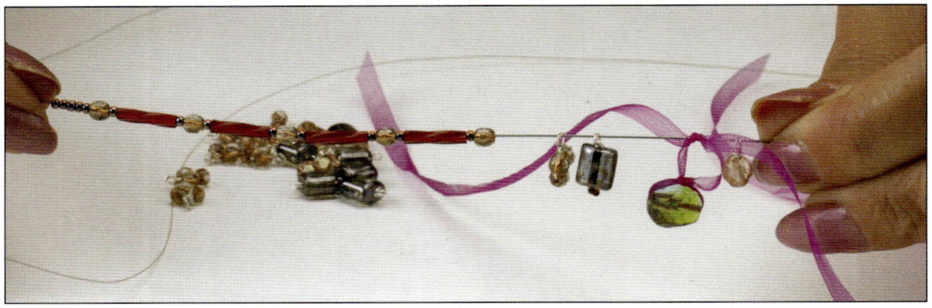

Add the bead drops and ribbon beads to the line, making sure to run the needle through the center of the ribbon knot to keep it from unraveling.

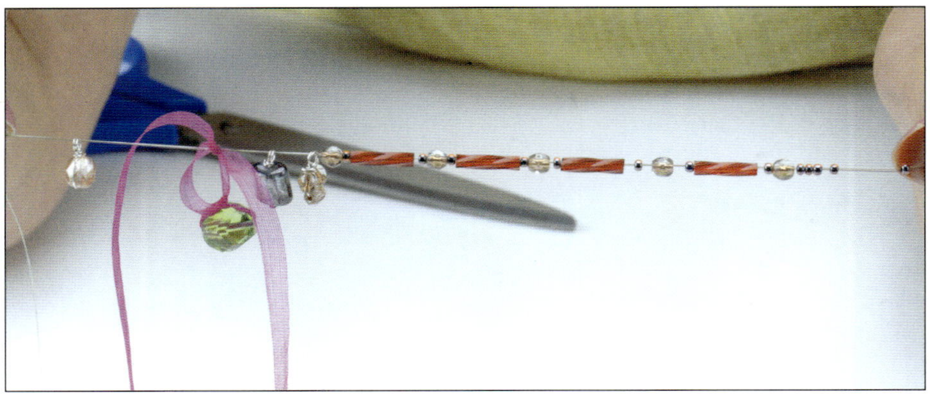

Another look at the sequence.

Run the line back thorough the little pink bead preceding the drops to draw all the drops and ribbon together in a cluster.

Threading the needle through the pink bead to create the next cluster of drops.

Pull the cluster tightly together as befor, and repeat this sequence seven times.

All seven of the clusters are now in place.

The necklace beading is complete.

Take a small piece of wire, fold it in half, and tie it securely to the end of the necklace. Tie the line twice to make sure the wire is secure.

One more knot to secure the wire.

Snug the cone down tightly and add a short chain for the clasp.

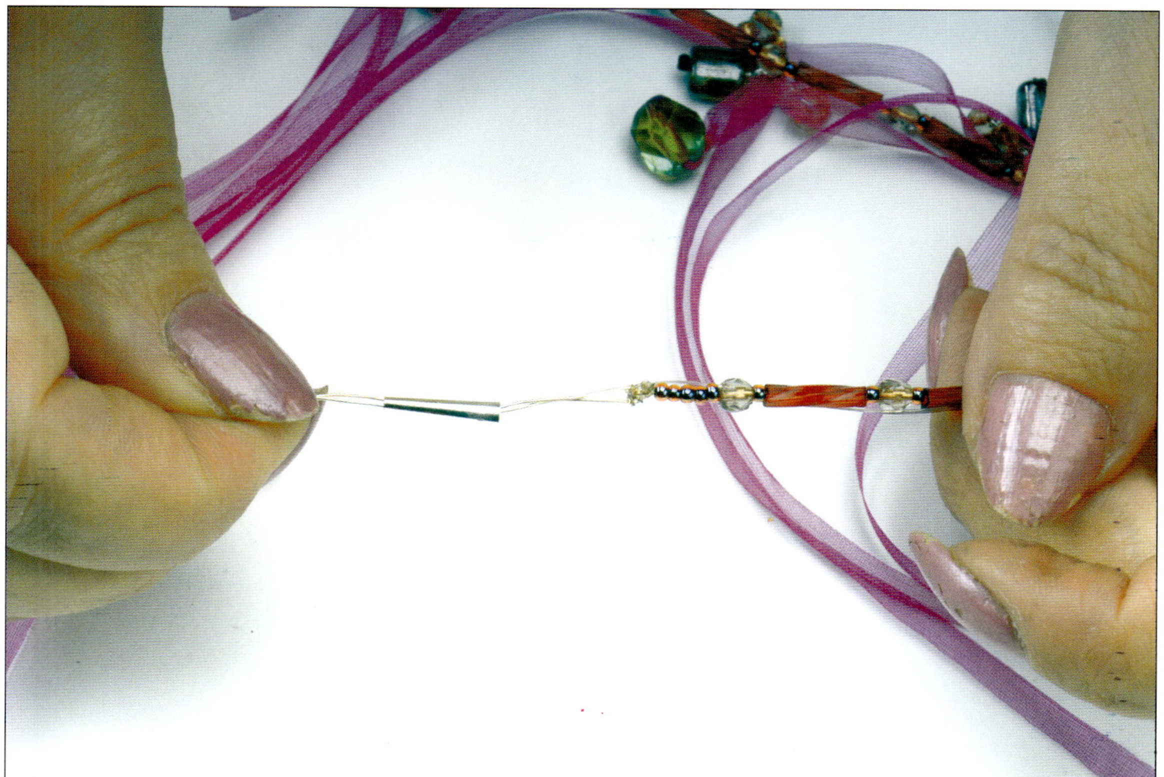

Place the cone over the folded wire…

Use the round nosed pliers to make a loop with the wire.

Snip off the excess wire.

Wrap the wire up the cone several times.

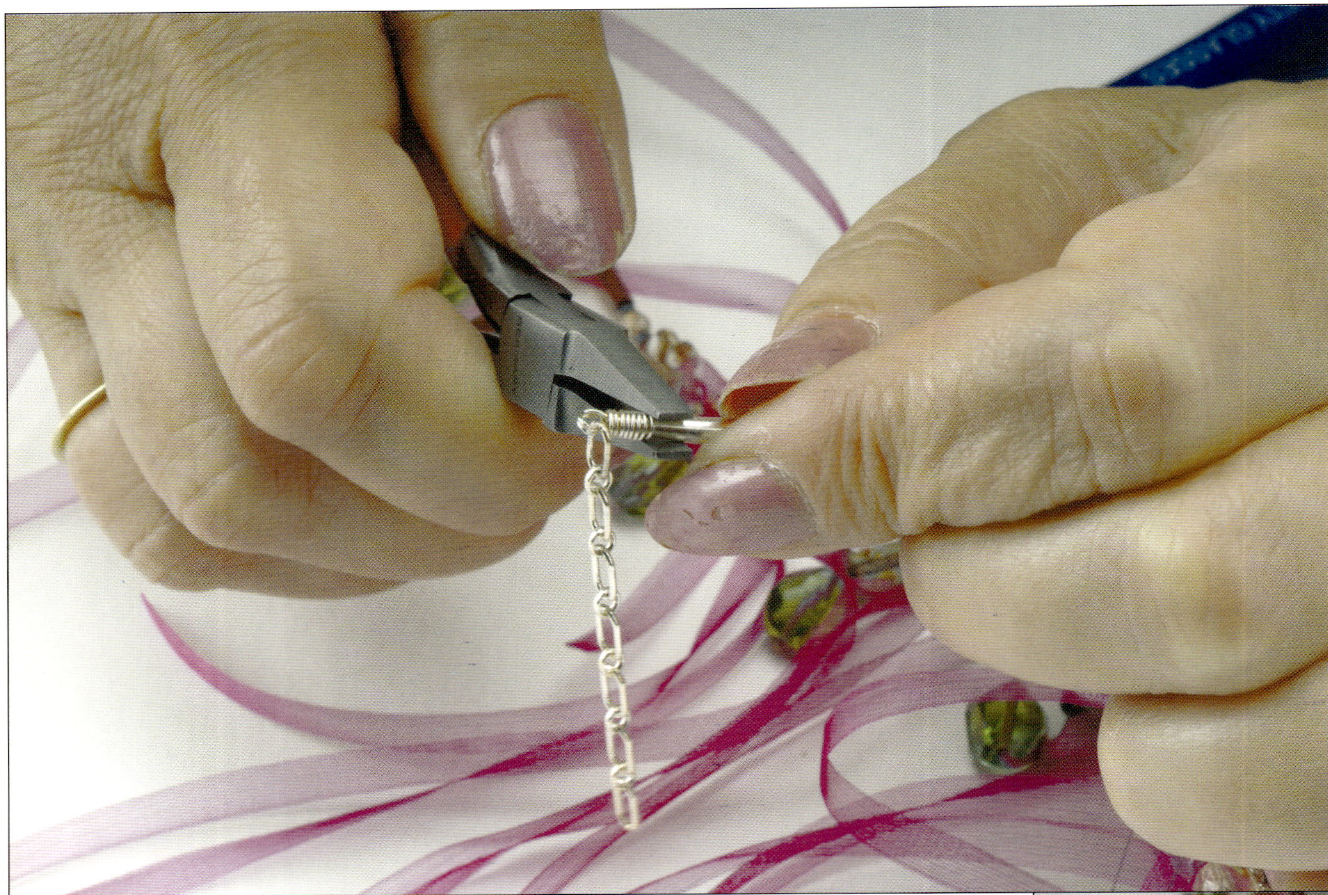

Flatten the end of the wire where the cut was made.

Cut off the excess thread.

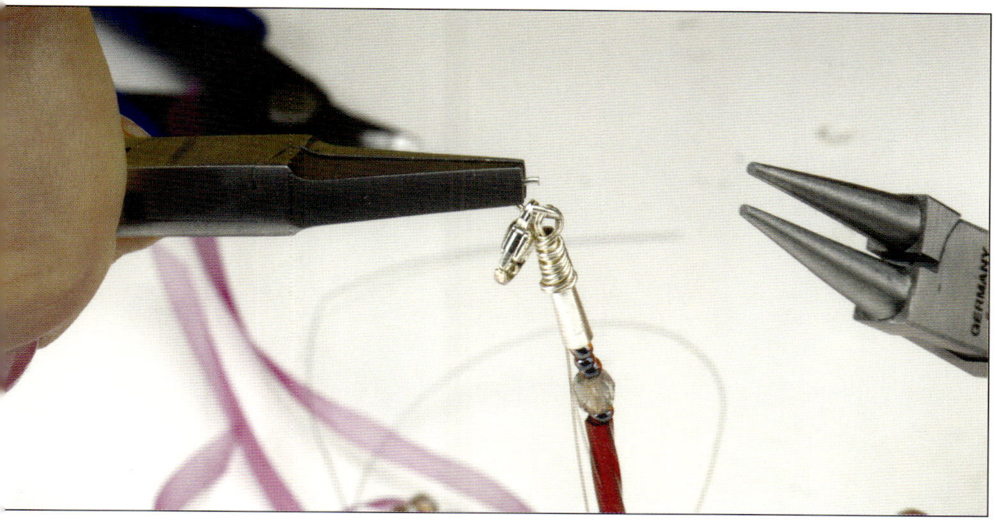

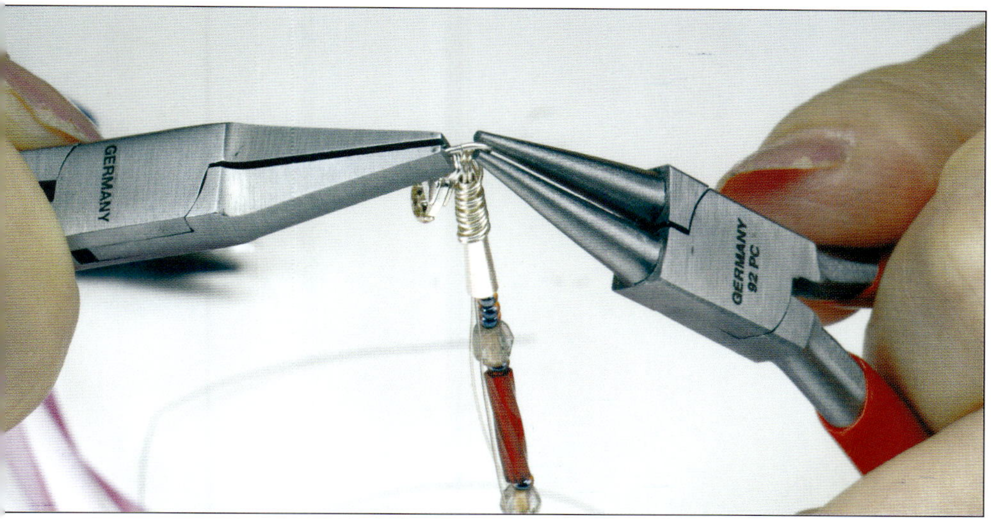

Add the clasp to the other end of the necklace.

Adding the end bead to the chain as a finishing touch.

The completed necklace.

Cropped Ribbon Necklace

We are making a beaded choker with long ribbons all around that can be cut short for a more classic look.

Here is the bead color palette and the black organza ribbon used for the next necklace. The ribbon is 5mm wide and may be hard to get.

Begin by threading the ribbon on your needle and threading twenty-five beads on the ribbon.

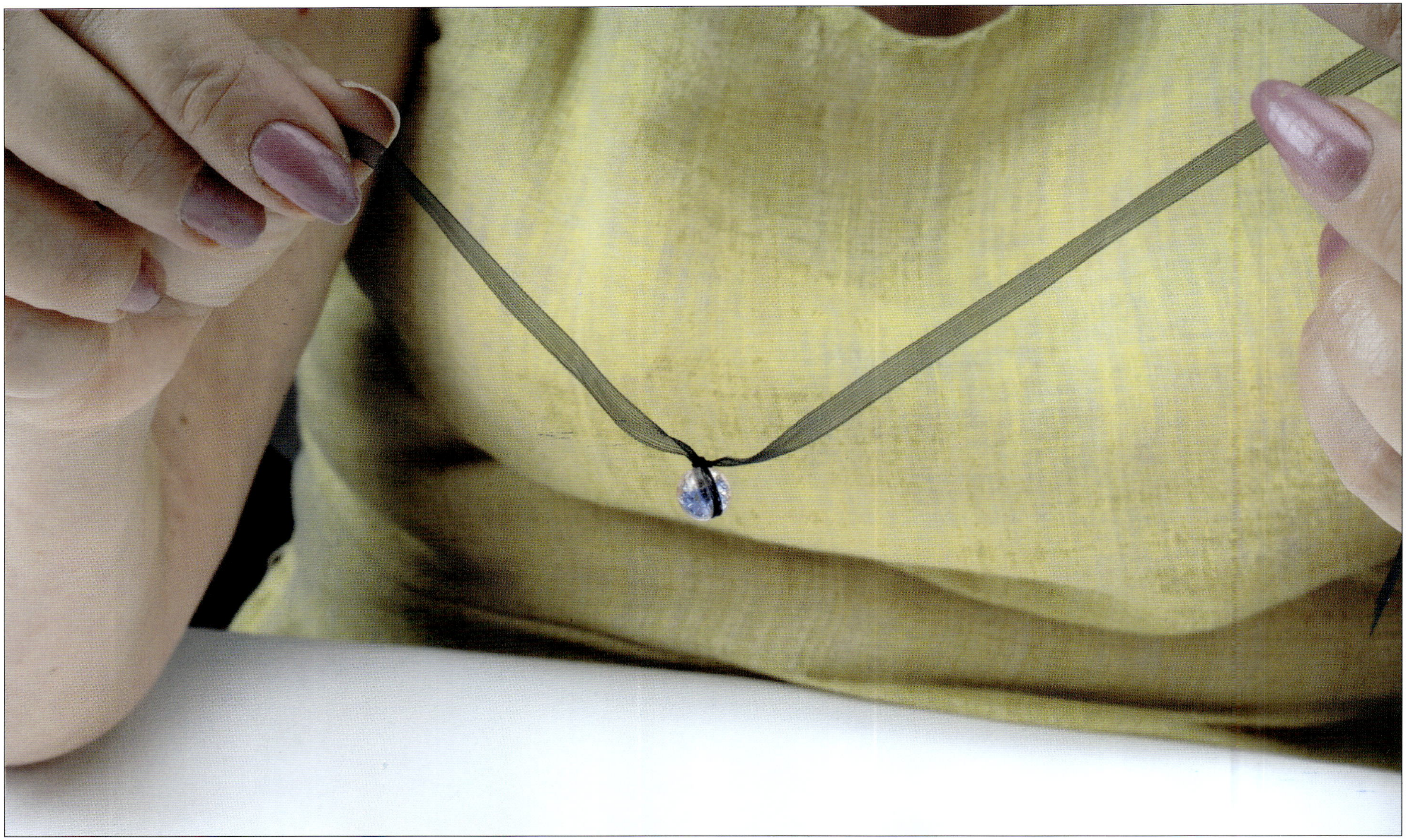

Knot each of the twenty-five beads to the ribbon and then cut the ribbon loose. Keep each ribbon uniform in length as you go. Cut the ribbon on a diagonal so it will not fray at the ends.

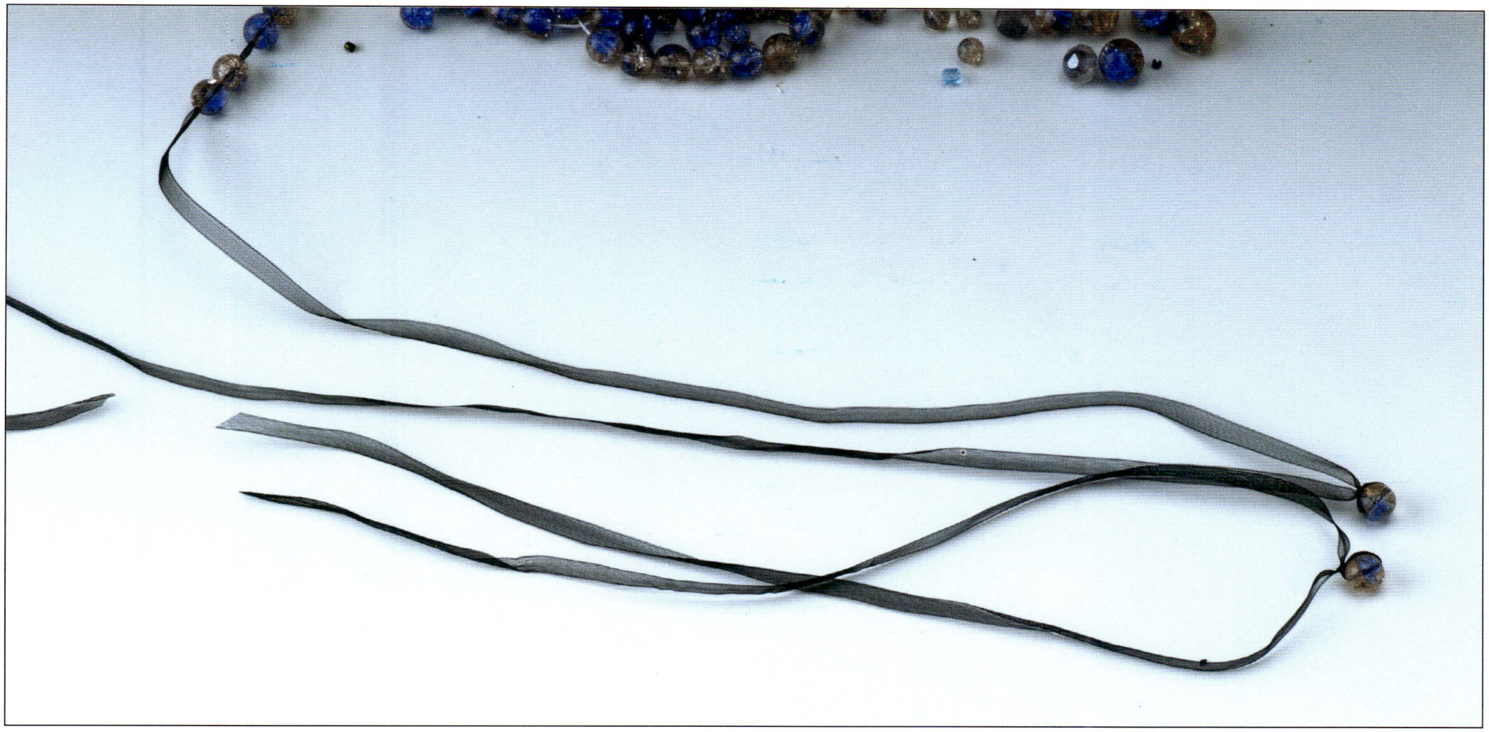

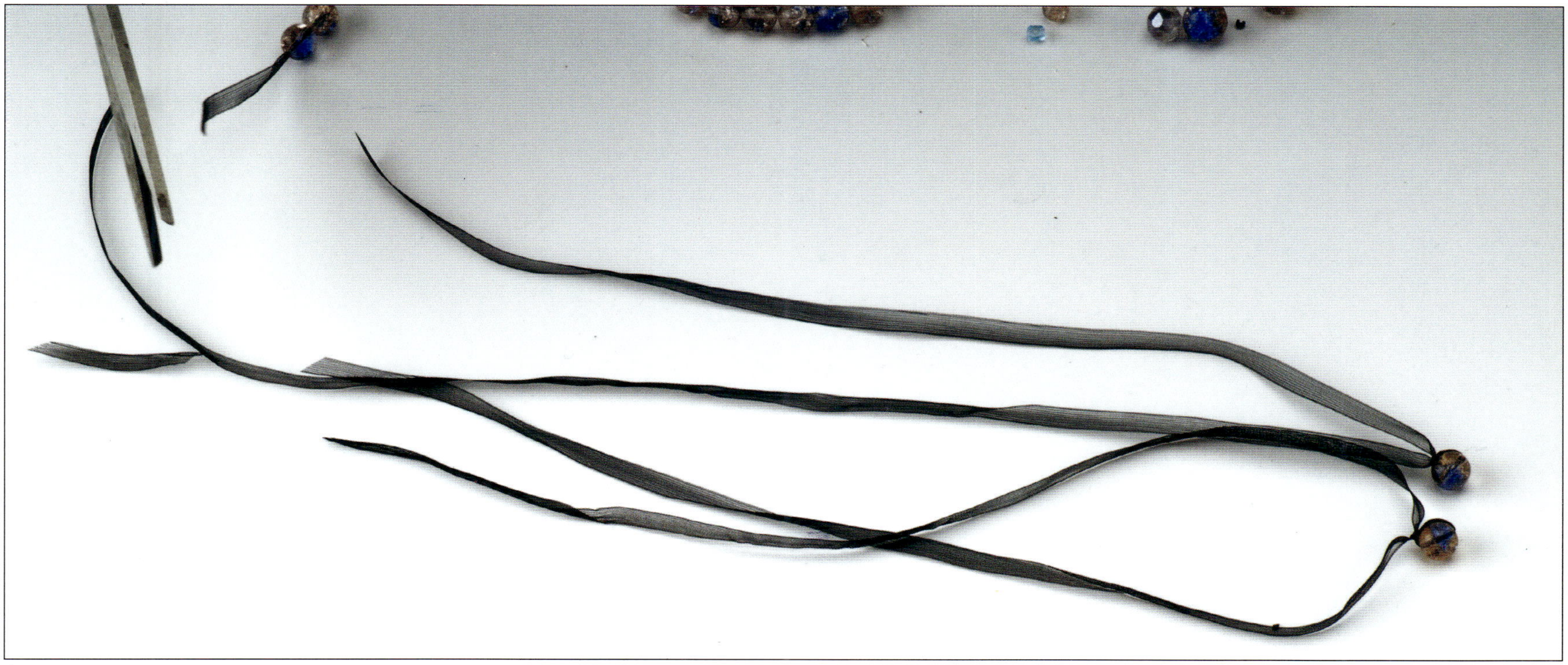

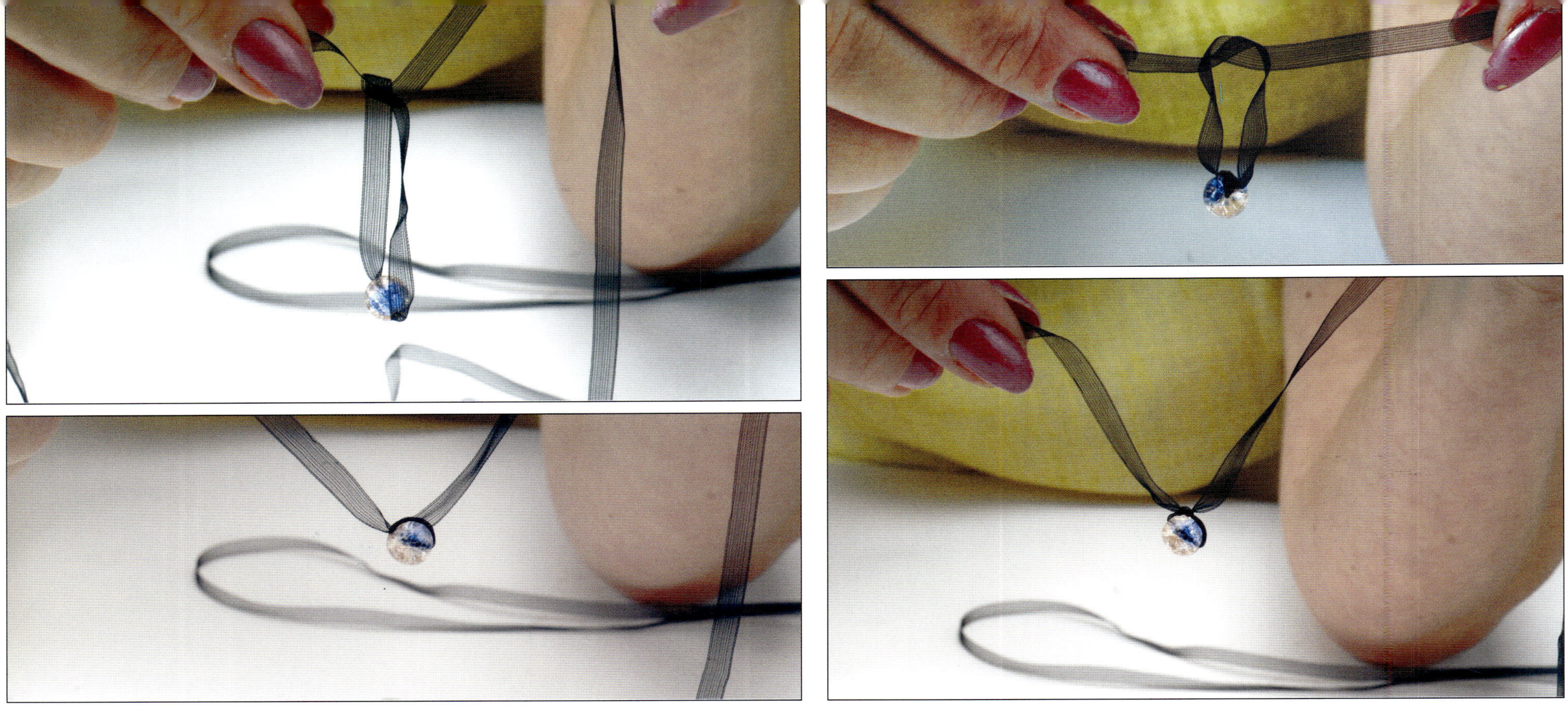

Continue knotting each bead to a length of ribbon. Double knot each bead in place to make sure it is secure.

All twenty-five beads are now attached to ribbons.

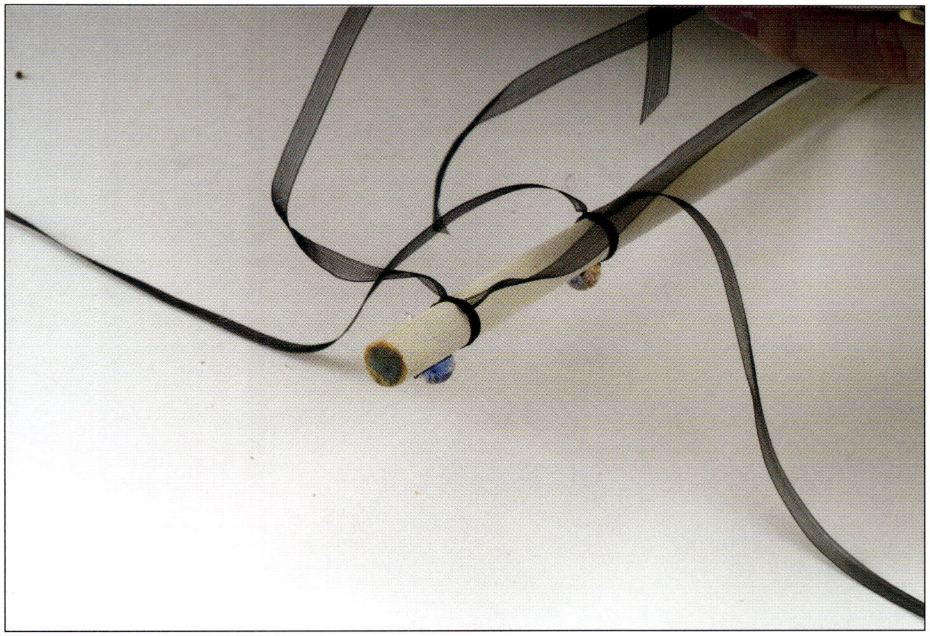

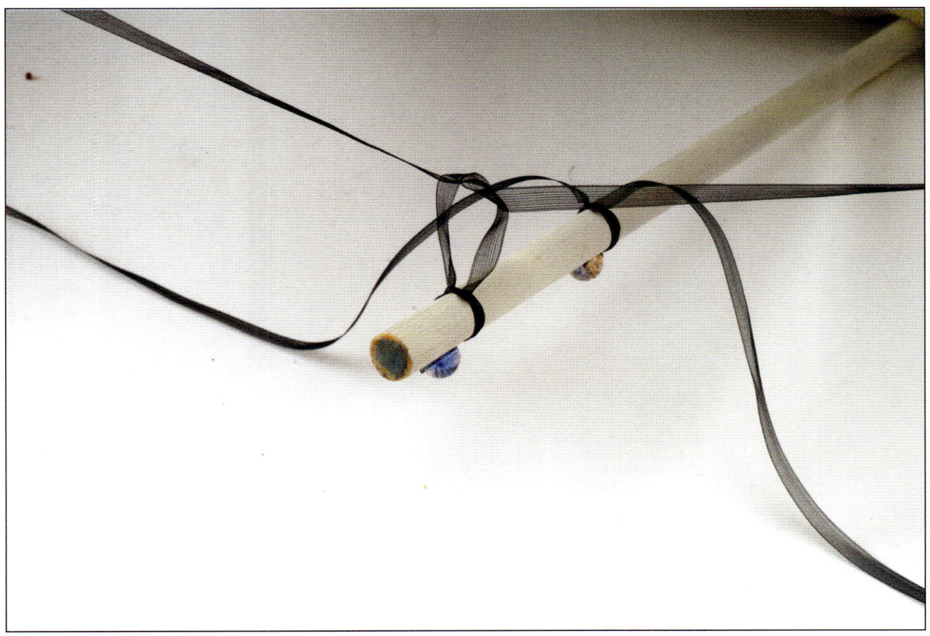

Now carefully tie the ribbons to a dowel. Double knot each ribbon tightly.

All the beads are now attached to the dowel.

Now carefully slide the beaded ribbons off the dowel.

Using a threaded needle, and making sure you knot the bottom end of the thread, first add seven beads to the thread, leaving about 5" extra to use to attach the clasps.

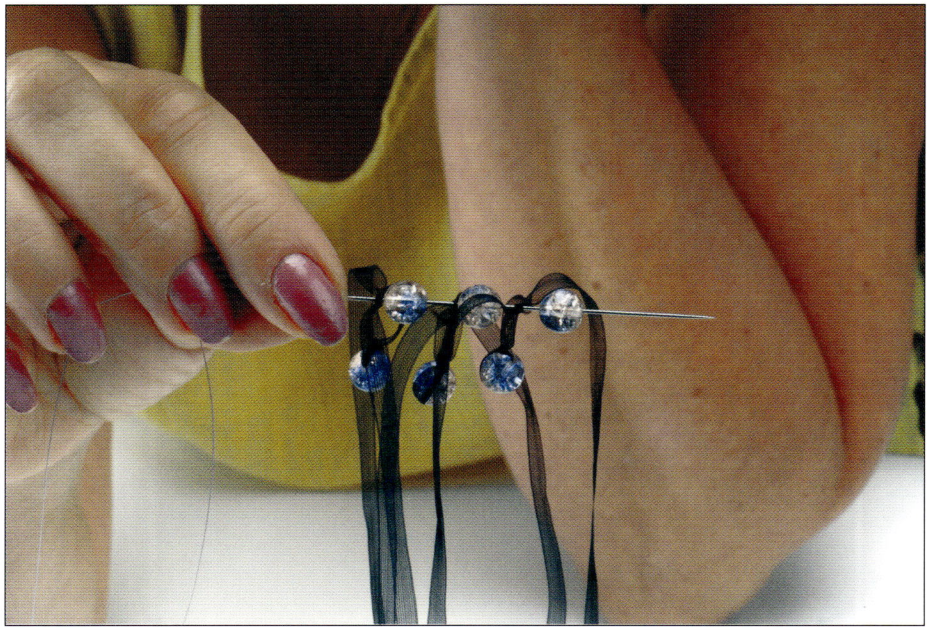

Now we start adding the ribbons. The needle must pass through the middle of the top knot. This is very important. Each beaded ribbon is separated by a single bead.

Progress. The thread passes right through the center of the ribbon knot.

The beading of the necklace is complete.

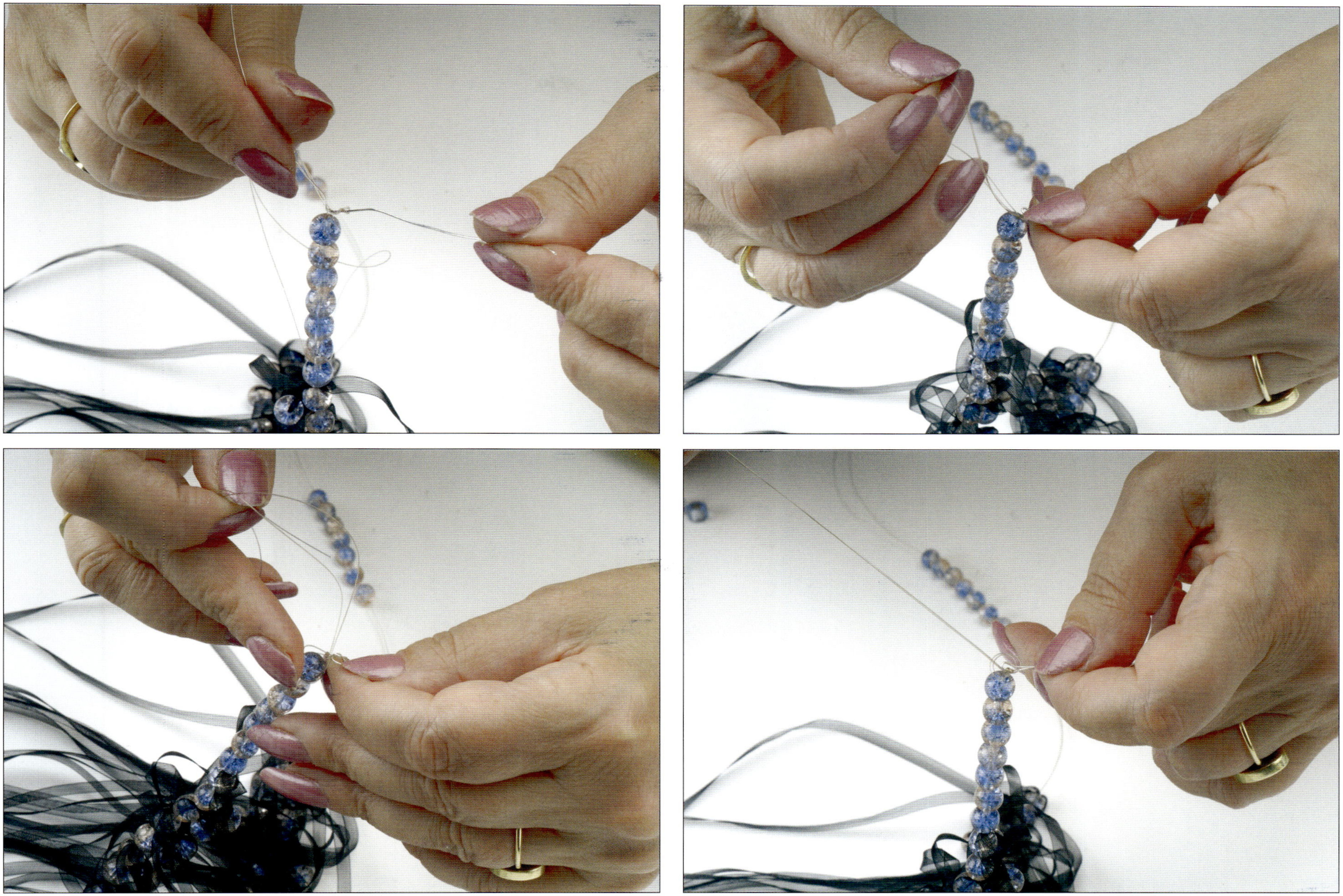

Fold a length of wire in half and attach it to one end of the necklace. To secure the wire in place, tie the monofilament to the wire twice and then loop a length of monofilament around one half of the wire to secure it in place.

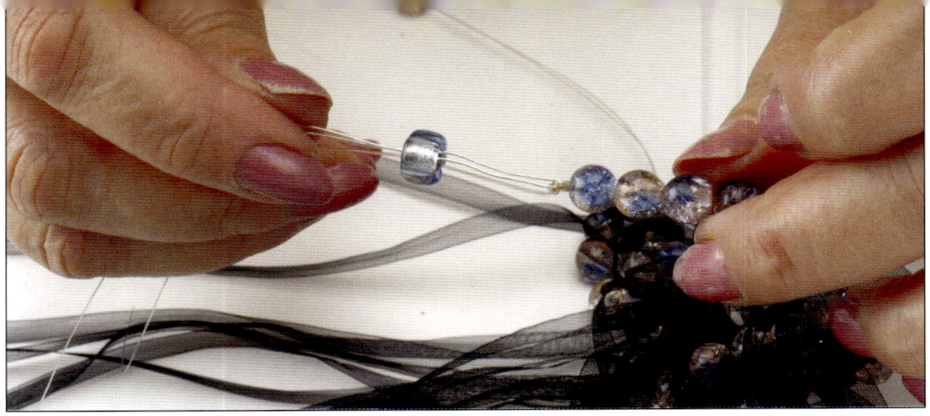

Take a bead with a big hole and thread it through the monofilament and the folded wire.

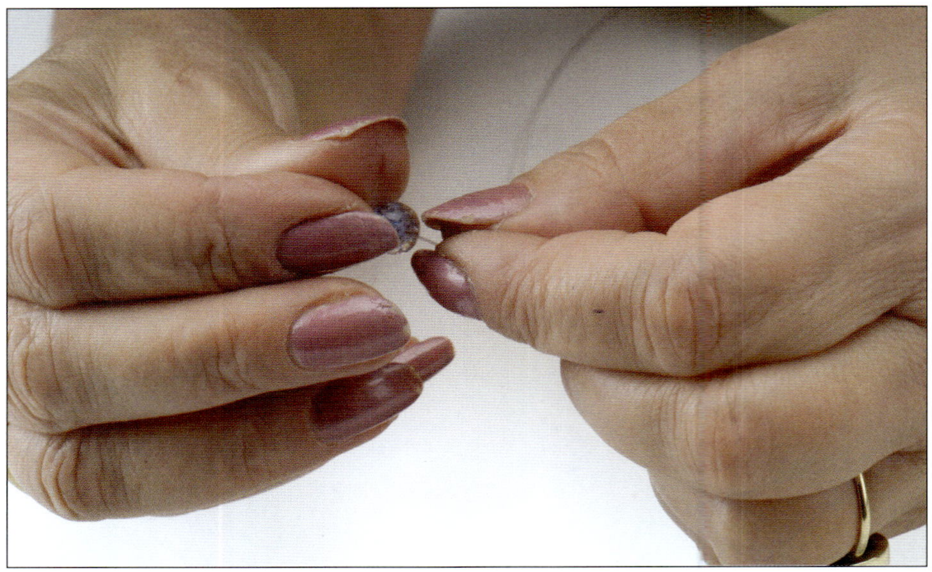

Thread a second bead through the monofilament and wire and push it down tightly against the preceding bead and the necklace.

Pull the two beads down tight, use the round nosed pliers to make a loop.

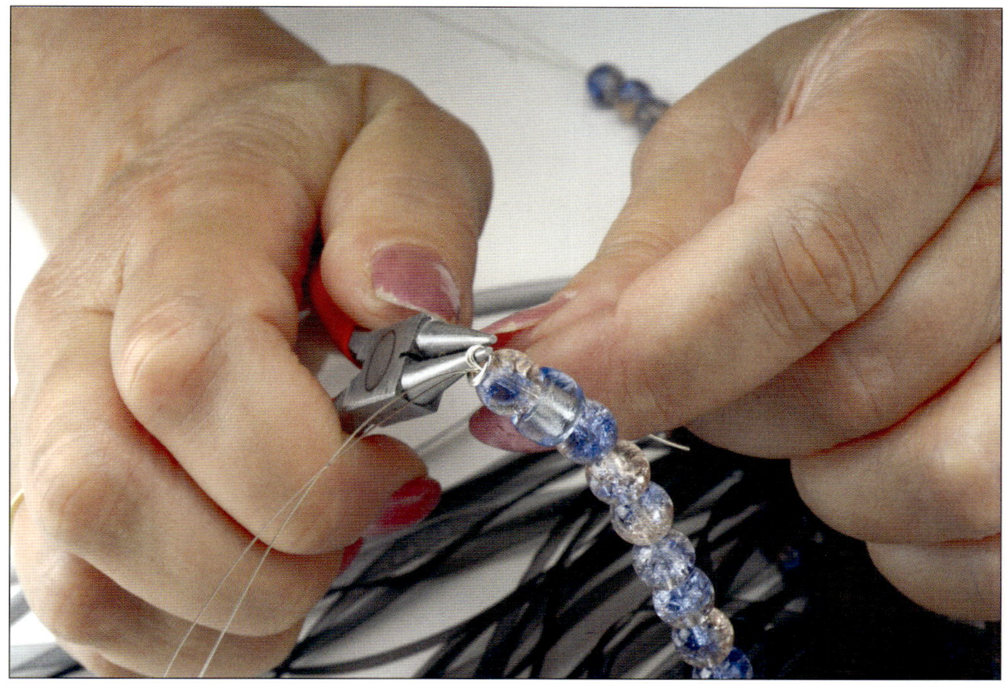

Cut away the excess monofilament and wire.

Repeat these steps on the other end of the necklace. Both ends are now complete.

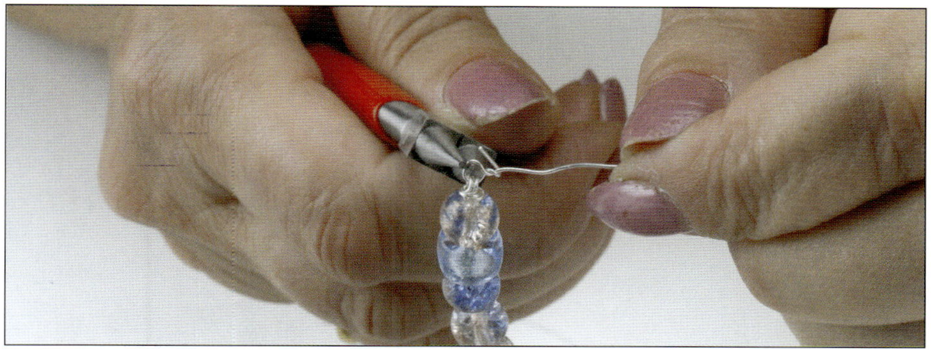

Using lengths of wire and the round nosed pliers, we will now make a beaded chain at the end of the necklace. Put wire through the loop at the end of the finished necklace and make a loop.

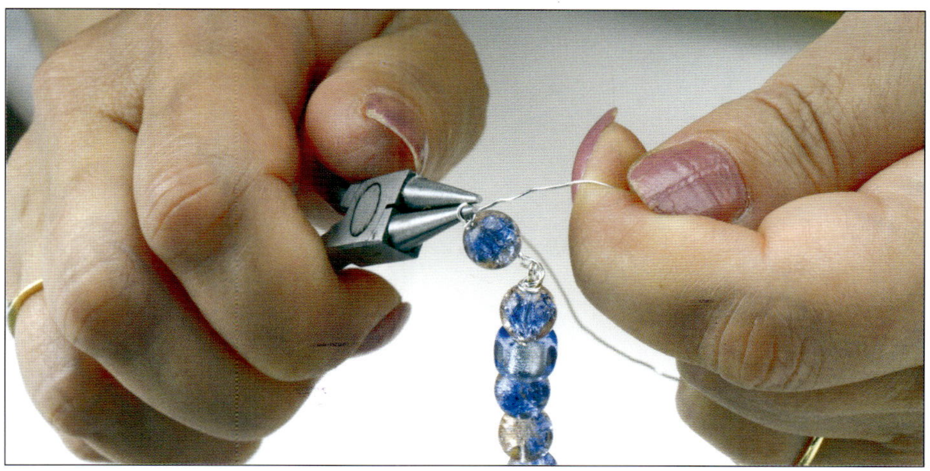

Add a bead and make another loop.

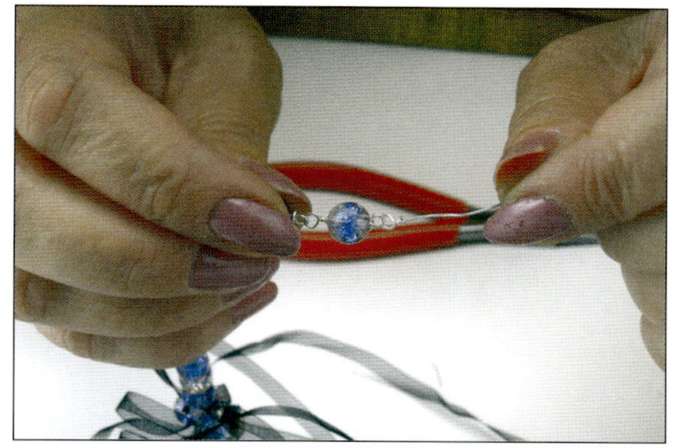

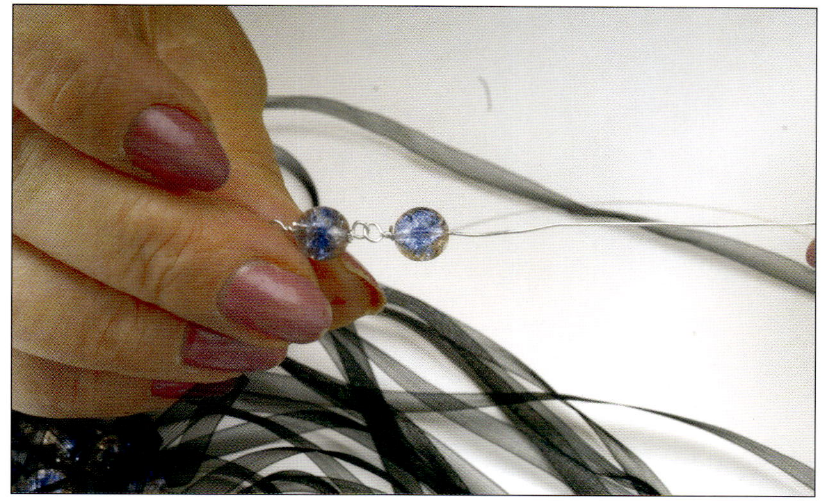

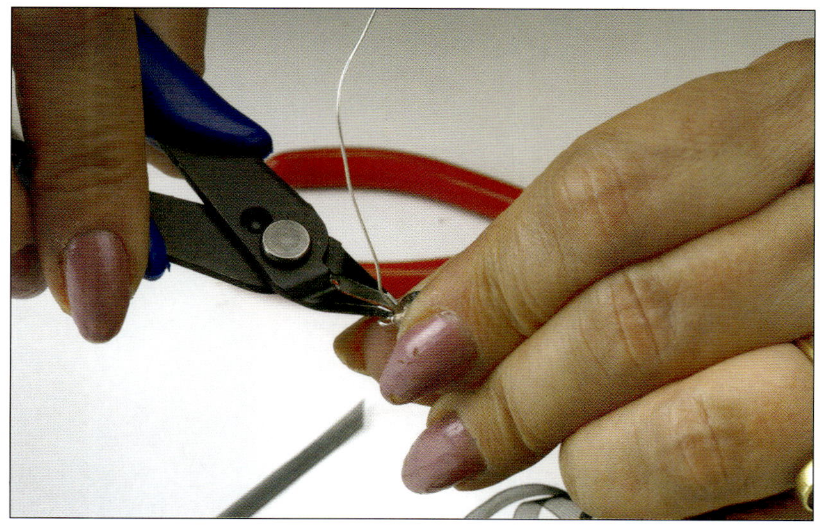

Repeat by putting wire through the loop to make a new loop, adding a bead and making another loop five times.

Now make the end bead, put a seed bead on the wire and fold in half. Thread the folded wire through the larger bead, pulling the seed bead up tight against the base to hold the wire in place. Attach this end bead to the head chain as before.

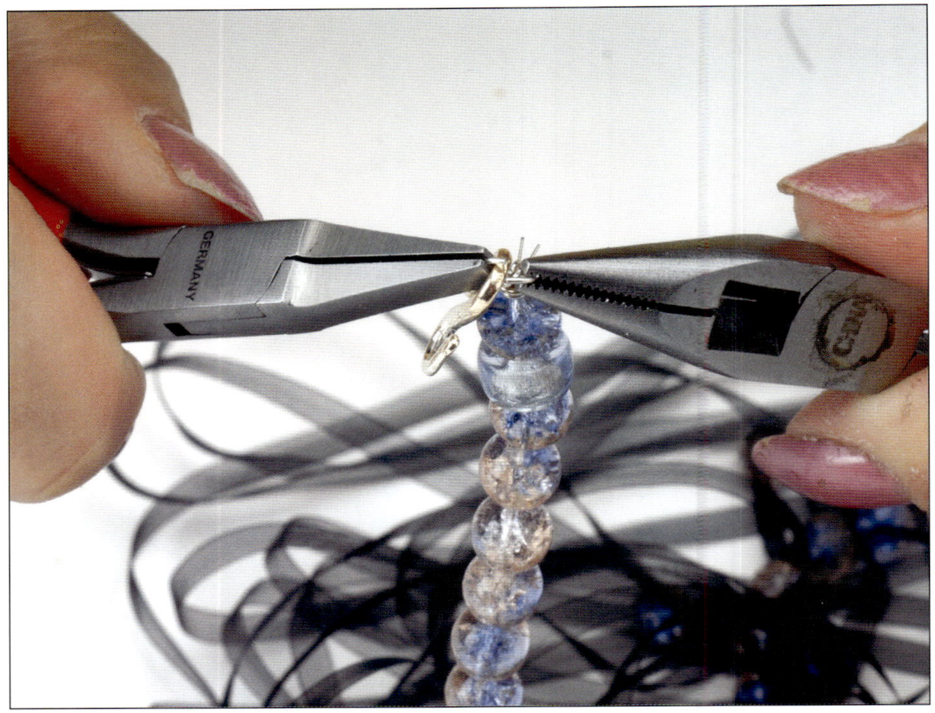

Attach the S-hook to the other end of the necklace with pliers and the small jump ring.

Trim the ribbons to length.

Always trim the ribbons on the diagonal so they will not fray.

The necklace is complete and the ribbons are of even length.

You can make a completely different necklace by cutting these ribbons very short.

The new look for the necklace with the short ribbons is complete.
If this is the look you want, you can start cutting the ribbons short from the beginning; this will save some ribbon.

Beaded Drop Earrings

Now, with a few drops, we can make earrings. Thread these drops (the same as in the necklace) onto 26-gauge wire.

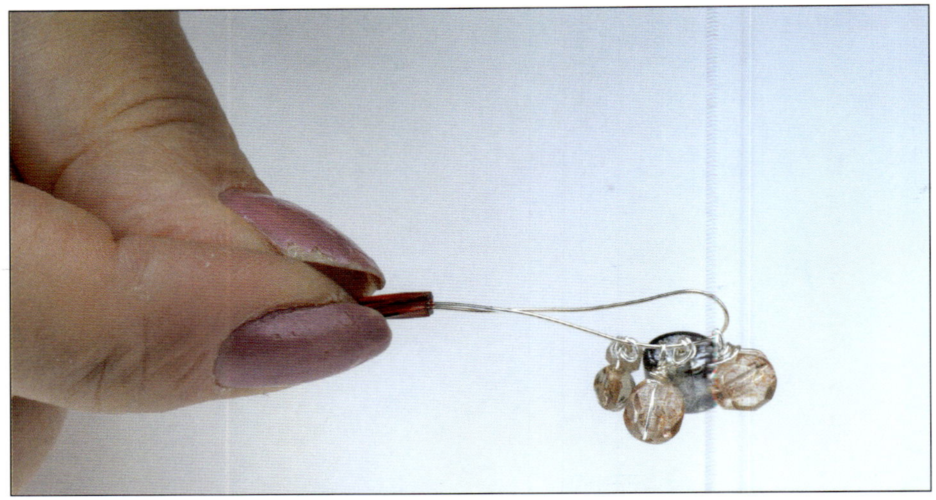

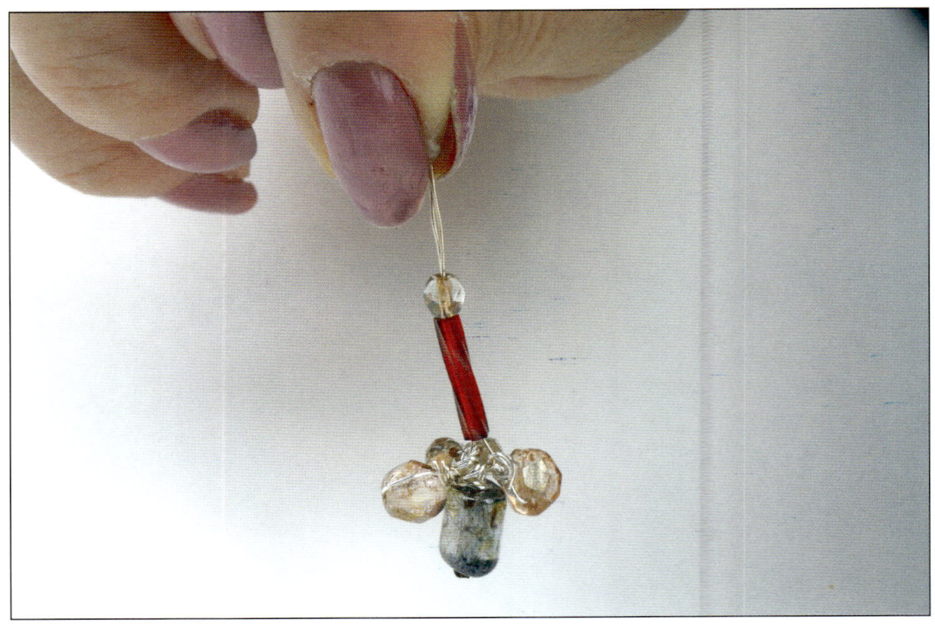

Fold the wire in half and put both ends through a long bead.

Use the round nosed pliers to create a loop, following the same techniques as before.

Clip loose the excess wire.

Use pliers to attach the earring to the ear wire.

The earrings are complete.

Kits are available from the author with all the items you'll need to make these projects. When you purchase the kits, the drops come preassembled.

You may order kits from the author for the beaded flower projects.

Ani Afshar's Beaded Fantasies Gallery

Necklace

Necklace

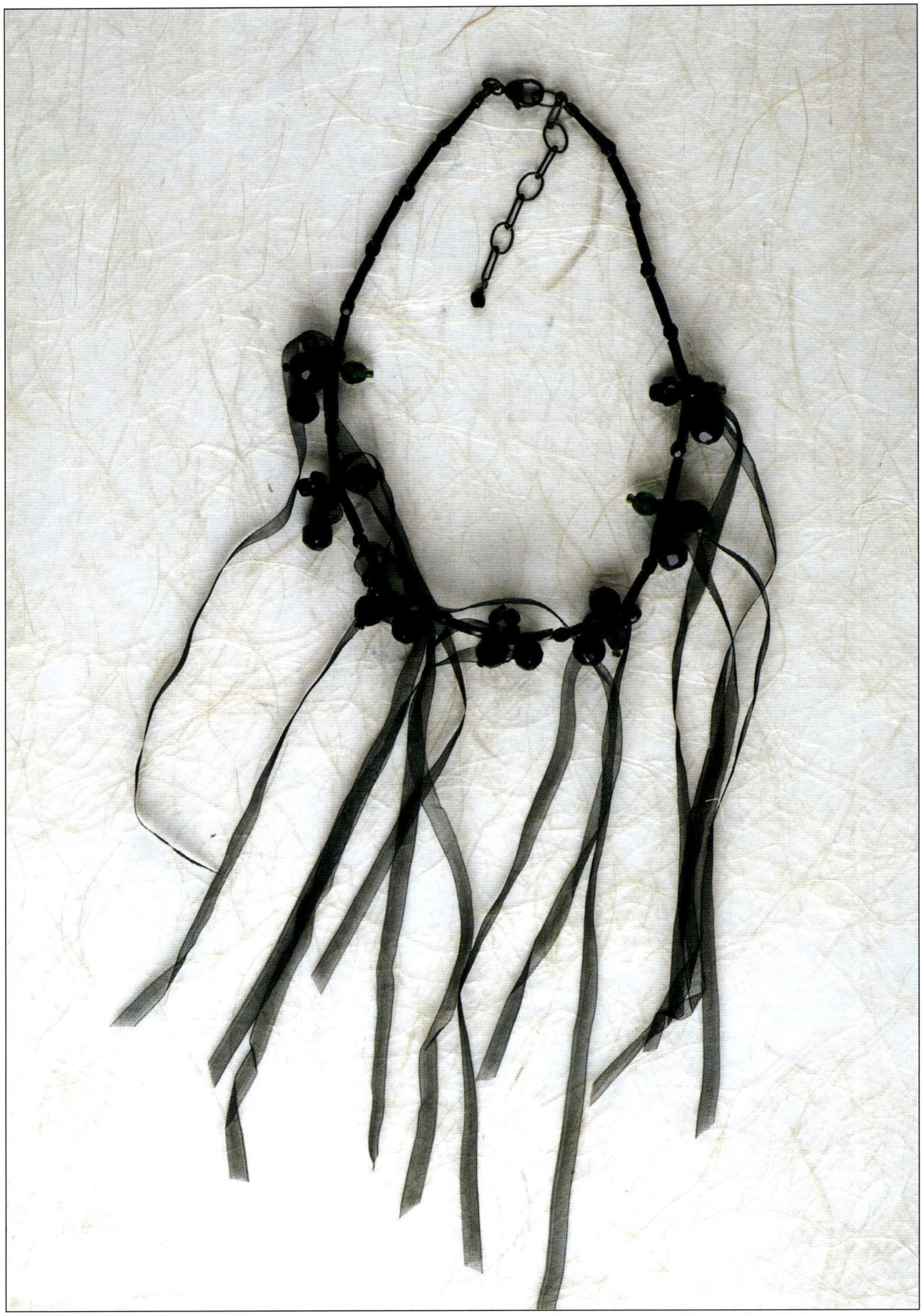

Necklaces

Necklace

Necklaces

Necklaces

Necklace

Bracelet